DATE DUE			

BC 9297

796.332 Gibbons, Gail
GIB

My football book

Meadowview Elementary School
1879 Wee Kirk Road
Atlanta, GA 30316

Bound to Stay Bound Books, Inc.

GAIL GIBBONS

MY FOOTBALL

BOOK

HarperCollinsPublishers

Special thanks to Frank Price, consultant,
for his expert review of the text and
illustrations in this book.

My Football Book
Copyright © 2000 by Gail Gibbons
Printed in Singapore at Tien Wah Press.
All rights reserved.
www.harperchildrens.com
Library of Congress Cataloging-in-Publication Data
Gibbons, Gail.
My football book / Gail Gibbons.—
1st ed.
p cm.
ISBN 0-688-17139-7
1. Football—Juvenile literature.   I. Title.   GV950.7.G52 2000
99-87202
10 9 8 7 6 5 4
❖

Football is fun, whether you are playing yourself or rooting for your favorite team. To play, you need a ball, protective gear, and sometimes a uniform.

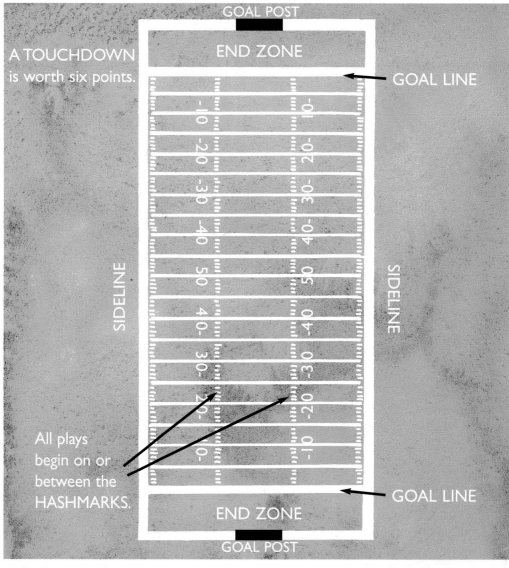

A football game is played on a football field.

Each team puts eleven players on the field, who work together to score the most points. The best way to score is to put the ball into the other team's end zone. That's a touchdown!

WIDE RECEIVER

TACKLE

GUARD

RUNNING BACKS

CENTER

QUARTERBACK

GUARD

TACKLE

TIGHT END

WIDE RECEIVER

LINEMEN

Each team has plans of action called plays. For different plays, the players have different jobs. The team on offense is the one that has the ball.

The COACH guides his or her team.

LINEBACKERS

DEFENSIVE BACKS

The team on defense tries to stop the other team from scoring.

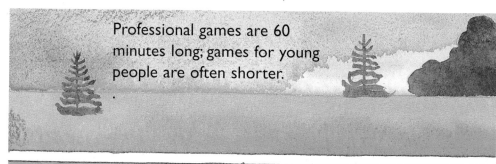

Professional games are 60 minutes long; games for young people are often shorter.

The REFEREE makes sure the game is played fairly.

Games are divided into four quarters. To begin the game, the referee tosses a coin. The team that wins the toss has the choice of receiving the ball or defending a certain end zone.

Professional games kick off at the 30 yard line.

TEE

The Rockets win the toss. They choose to receive the ball. The Dragons line up on the 40 yard line. A special kicker comes out for the kickoff. The ball goes deep into Rocket territory.

When defensive players stop the offensive ball carrier, it is called a TACKLE.

A Rocket catches the ball. He runs toward Dragon territory, but the Dragons stop him.

In a HUDDLE, a team groups together to get instructions from the quarterback, team captain, or coach.

Now the Rockets have four plays, called downs, to move the ball ten yards toward the Dragon end zone. If they succeed, they'll get four more plays. The team goes into a huddle.

The place where the ball rests on the field is called the LINE OF SCRIMMAGE.

Ready...

The Rocket quarterback calls the first play. The teams line up at the line of scrimmage. The quarterback yells, "Ready...set...hut...hut...hike!" The center snaps the ball to the quarterback.

The quarterback passes the football to a Rocket teammate. The player runs two yards and is quickly tackled. The Rockets are second down and eight, which means they have three chances left and eight more yards to go.

In four downs, the Rockets have gained ten yards.
Now they get to keep the ball for four more plays.

A FIELD GOAL is made when a special kicker comes out and kicks the ball through the uprights of the goal post. It's worth three points.

The game continues. The Rockets make it to the Dragon 15 yard line with one down to go. They decide to try a field goal instead of a fourth play.

The kick isn't good. Now it's the Dragons' ball. The teams scrimmage. The Dragon center snaps the ball to the quarterback, who passes it to a teammate.

A PENALTY is given when a rule is broken.

The referee tosses a yellow flag. A Dragon player moved before the ball was put into play. There's a penalty. The Dragons have to move back five yards.

The score is Dragons 7, Rockets 0.

But the Dragons are fast. At last a Dragon player carries the ball across the Rocket goal line. Touchdown—that's six points! Now the Dragons get to try for an extra point. A special kicker comes out, and he makes it.

After the first quarter the teams change sides.
When the second quarter has been played, it's
halftime. The score is still Dragons 7, Rockets 0.

Halftime is over. The teams switch sides again and go back into action. There's another kickoff to start play.

For two more quarters the players pass, run, tackle, and kick.

There are only a few seconds left in the game. The score is tied at 14 points. The Rockets try for one last field goal. BOOM . . .

and it's in for three points! The final score is
Rockets 17, Dragons 14. Everybody cheers because
it's been such a good game.

MY FOOTBALL GLOSSARY

OFFENSIVE PLAYERS

The **quarterback** calls signals, throws passes, hands off the ball, and runs the ball.

The **offensive linemen** (the center, guards, and tackles) block defenders from getting the ball.

Running backs often take the ball from the quarterback and run toward the opposite team's goal. They can also catch or pass the ball as they run.

Tight ends block and catch the ball.

Wide receivers block and catch passes.

DEFENSIVE PLAYERS

Defensive linemen try to stop all movement toward their team's goal.

Linebackers are the most athletic players. They try to stop runs, rush the quarterback, and stop passes.

Defensive backs are in charge of stopping receivers from catching the ball.

OTHER DEFINITIONS

block: to stop an opponent from tackling a team member who has the ball

defense: working to prevent the offense from scoring by tackling, intercepting the ball, and other means

fumble: when a player drops the ball

offense: working to score points by kicking, passing, and running with the ball

punting the ball: If the offense hasn't gained ten yards in three downs, it can choose to kick the ball deep into an opponent's territory.

sportsmanship: playing fairly and enjoying the game, no matter who wins or loses

teamwork: playing together as a team, encouraging and suppporting all of your teammates